50 Dishes to Dance For

By: Kelly Johnson

Table of Contents

- Salsa Verde Chicken Enchiladas
- Spicy Shrimp Tacos
- Mango Chili Glazed Salmon
- Crispy Fried Chicken
- Jerk Pork with Coconut Rice
- Beef Empanadas
- BBQ Ribs with Honey Jalapeño Sauce
- Banh Mi Sandwiches
- Pad Thai
- Sizzling Fajitas
- Lobster Roll
- Lamb Kofta with Tzatziki
- Tempura Vegetables
- Sweet and Sour Pork
- Fish and Chips
- Chicken Shawarma
- Grilled Lamb Chops with Mint Yogurt

- Jambalaya
- Beef Bulgogi
- Duck Confit with Orange Sauce
- Tandoori Chicken
- Peking Duck
- Korean BBQ Beef
- Moussaka
- Paella
- Crab Cakes with Lemon Aioli
- Chicken Parmesan
- Grilled Octopus with Lemon
- Thai Green Curry
- Stuffed Grape Leaves
- Beef Wellington
- Shrimp Scampi
- Chimichurri Steak
- Lamb Tagine
- Chicken Kiev
- Baked Ziti

- Risotto with Porcini Mushrooms
- Porchetta
- Lobster Bisque
- Prawn Ceviche
- Tofu Stir-Fry
- Grilled Vegetable Skewers
- Pulled Pork Sandwiches
- Spaghetti Carbonara
- Veal Piccata
- Chili Crab
- Beef Rendang
- Baked Cod with Lemon and Capers
- Pappardelle with Duck Ragu
- Sautéed Scallops with Garlic Butter

Salsa Verde Chicken Enchiladas

Ingredients:

For the enchiladas:

- 3 cups cooked chicken (shredded)
- 1 cup salsa verde
- 10 corn tortillas
- 1 cup shredded cheddar cheese
- 1/2 cup sour cream
- 1/2 tsp cumin
- 1/2 tsp garlic powder
- Salt and pepper to taste

For garnish:

- Fresh cilantro
- Diced red onion

Instructions:

1. Preheat your oven to 375°F (190°C).
2. In a bowl, mix shredded chicken, salsa verde, cumin, garlic powder, salt, and pepper.
3. Lightly warm the tortillas to make them pliable.

4. Scoop a generous portion of the chicken mixture into each tortilla and roll them up tightly.

5. Place the rolled tortillas seam side down in a baking dish.

6. Pour the remaining salsa verde over the top and sprinkle with shredded cheddar cheese.

7. Bake for 20-25 minutes until the cheese is melted and bubbly.

8. Garnish with sour cream, cilantro, and diced red onion before serving.

Spicy Shrimp Tacos

Ingredients:

For the shrimp:

- 1 lb shrimp (peeled and deveined)
- 1 tbsp olive oil
- 1 tbsp chili powder
- 1/2 tsp cumin
- 1/2 tsp smoked paprika
- 1/2 tsp garlic powder
- Salt and pepper to taste

For the taco toppings:

- 1/2 cup shredded cabbage
- 1/4 cup chopped cilantro
- 1/4 cup diced red onion
- 1 lime (cut into wedges)
- 8 small soft corn tortillas
- 1/4 cup sour cream
- 1 tbsp sriracha sauce (optional)

Instructions:

1. In a bowl, combine the olive oil, chili powder, cumin, smoked paprika, garlic powder, salt, and pepper.

2. Toss the shrimp in the spice mixture until well-coated.

3. Heat a large skillet over medium heat and cook the shrimp for 2-3 minutes per side until pink and cooked through.

4. Warm the tortillas in a dry skillet or microwave.

5. To assemble the tacos, place a few shrimp in each tortilla and top with shredded cabbage, cilantro, and red onion.

6. Drizzle sour cream mixed with sriracha sauce over the top, if desired.

7. Serve with lime wedges on the side for squeezing.

Mango Chili Glazed Salmon

Ingredients:

For the glaze:

- 1 ripe mango (peeled and diced)
- 1 tbsp chili paste or sriracha sauce
- 1 tbsp honey
- 1 tbsp lime juice
- 1/2 tsp soy sauce

For the salmon:

- 4 salmon fillets
- Salt and pepper to taste
- 1 tbsp olive oil

Instructions:

1. In a blender or food processor, blend the mango, chili paste, honey, lime juice, and soy sauce until smooth.
2. Season the salmon fillets with salt and pepper.
3. Heat the olive oil in a skillet over medium-high heat and cook the salmon for 3-4 minutes per side until golden and cooked through.
4. Brush the mango chili glaze over the salmon fillets during the last minute of cooking.
5. Serve the salmon with extra glaze on top.

Crispy Fried Chicken

Ingredients:

- 4 chicken thighs (bone-in, skin-on)
- 1 cup buttermilk
- 1 tbsp hot sauce
- 1 cup all-purpose flour
- 1 tbsp garlic powder
- 1 tbsp paprika
- 1/2 tsp cayenne pepper
- Salt and pepper to taste
- Vegetable oil (for frying)

Instructions:

1. In a bowl, combine the buttermilk and hot sauce. Submerge the chicken thighs in the mixture and refrigerate for at least 1 hour.
2. In a separate bowl, mix flour, garlic powder, paprika, cayenne, salt, and pepper.
3. Heat vegetable oil in a deep pan over medium-high heat to 350°F (175°C).
4. Dredge each chicken thigh in the flour mixture, making sure it is evenly coated.
5. Fry the chicken for 7-10 minutes per side until golden brown and cooked through.
6. Drain on paper towels and serve hot.

Jerk Pork with Coconut Rice

Ingredients:

For the jerk pork:

- 1 lb pork tenderloin (cut into 1-inch pieces)
- 2 tbsp jerk seasoning
- 1 tbsp olive oil
- 2 cloves garlic (minced)
- 1 tbsp soy sauce
- 1 tbsp lime juice

For the coconut rice:

- 1 cup jasmine rice
- 1 cup coconut milk
- 1 cup water
- 1 tbsp sugar
- Salt to taste

Instructions:

1. Toss the pork pieces in jerk seasoning, olive oil, garlic, soy sauce, and lime juice. Marinate for at least 30 minutes.

2. For the rice, combine the rice, coconut milk, water, sugar, and salt in a pot. Bring to a boil, then reduce heat and simmer, covered, for 15-20 minutes until the rice is tender.

3. Heat a skillet over medium-high heat and cook the pork for 5-7 minutes until browned and cooked through.

4. Serve the jerk pork over coconut rice, garnished with chopped cilantro.

Beef Empanadas

Ingredients:

For the filling:

- 1 lb ground beef
- 1 onion (chopped)
- 1/2 bell pepper (chopped)
- 2 cloves garlic (minced)
- 1 tsp cumin
- 1/2 tsp paprika
- Salt and pepper to taste
- 1/4 cup raisins (optional)
- 1/4 cup chopped olives (optional)

For the dough:

- 2 cups all-purpose flour
- 1/2 tsp salt
- 1/2 cup cold butter (cubed)
- 1 egg (beaten)
- 1/4 cup cold water

Instructions:

1. In a skillet, brown the ground beef with onions, bell pepper, and garlic. Add cumin, paprika, salt, pepper, raisins, and olives. Cook for another 2 minutes.

2. For the dough, mix flour and salt in a bowl. Add cubed butter and rub it in with your fingers until the mixture resembles coarse crumbs.

3. Add the egg and cold water, mixing until the dough forms. Wrap in plastic and chill for 30 minutes.

4. Preheat your oven to 375°F (190°C). Roll out the dough and cut into circles.

5. Place a spoonful of the beef mixture in the center of each dough circle. Fold over and seal the edges with a fork.

6. Bake the empanadas for 20-25 minutes until golden brown.

BBQ Ribs with Honey Jalapeño Sauce

Ingredients:

For the ribs:

- 2 racks of baby back ribs
- 1/4 cup BBQ rub

For the sauce:

- 1/4 cup honey
- 1 tbsp olive oil
- 2 cloves garlic (minced)
- 2 tbsp apple cider vinegar
- 1-2 jalapeños (minced)
- 1/4 cup ketchup
- Salt and pepper to taste

Instructions:

1. Preheat your oven to 300°F (150°C). Rub the ribs with BBQ rub and wrap them in foil.
2. Bake for 2-3 hours until tender.
3. For the sauce, heat olive oil in a pan and sauté garlic and jalapeños for 2 minutes. Add honey, vinegar, ketchup, salt, and pepper, and simmer for 5 minutes.
4. Brush the sauce on the ribs and bake for another 10-15 minutes.

5. Serve with extra sauce on the side.

Banh Mi Sandwiches

Ingredients:

For the pickled vegetables:

- 1/2 cup julienned carrots
- 1/2 cup julienned daikon radish
- 1/4 cup rice vinegar
- 1 tbsp sugar
- 1/4 tsp salt

For the sandwiches:

- 4 baguettes or hoagie rolls
- 1 lb pork belly or grilled chicken, thinly sliced
- 1/4 cup cilantro leaves
- 1 cucumber, sliced
- 1/4 cup chopped chilies (optional)
- 1/4 cup mayonnaise
- 1 tbsp sriracha sauce (optional)

Instructions:

1. Make the pickled vegetables by mixing the rice vinegar, sugar, and salt. Add the carrots and radish and set aside for 30 minutes.

2. Mix mayonnaise and sriracha for the sandwich spread.

3. Slice the baguettes and toast lightly.

4. Assemble by spreading mayonnaise on each baguette, layering with pork or chicken, cucumber, cilantro, and pickled vegetables.

5. Garnish with optional chilies and serve immediately.

Pad Thai

Ingredients:

For the sauce:

- 3 tbsp fish sauce
- 1 tbsp soy sauce
- 1 tbsp lime juice
- 2 tbsp brown sugar
- 1 tbsp tamarind paste
- 1/2 tsp chili flakes (optional)

For the pad thai:

- 8 oz rice noodles
- 2 tbsp vegetable oil
- 1/2 lb shrimp, chicken, or tofu (optional)
- 2 eggs
- 1/2 cup bean sprouts
- 1/4 cup chopped green onions
- 1/4 cup chopped peanuts
- 1 lime (cut into wedges)

Instructions:

1. Cook the rice noodles according to package instructions, drain, and set aside.

2. In a small bowl, mix the fish sauce, soy sauce, lime juice, brown sugar, tamarind paste, and chili flakes to make the sauce.

3. Heat vegetable oil in a large pan over medium heat. Add the shrimp (or chicken/tofu) and cook until browned and cooked through. Remove from the pan.

4. In the same pan, scramble the eggs, then add the cooked noodles and sauce. Stir well.

5. Add the shrimp (or chicken/tofu), bean sprouts, and green onions, and stir to combine.

6. Serve with chopped peanuts and lime wedges on top.

Sizzling Fajitas

Ingredients:

For the marinade:

- 1/4 cup lime juice
- 1/4 cup olive oil
- 1 tbsp soy sauce
- 2 cloves garlic (minced)
- 1 tsp ground cumin
- 1 tsp chili powder
- Salt and pepper to taste

For the fajitas:

- 1 lb flank steak or chicken breasts
- 1 red bell pepper (sliced)
- 1 green bell pepper (sliced)
- 1 onion (sliced)
- 8 flour tortillas
- Optional toppings: sour cream, guacamole, salsa, shredded cheese

Instructions:

1. Combine lime juice, olive oil, soy sauce, garlic, cumin, chili powder, salt, and pepper in a bowl. Marinate the meat for at least 30 minutes.

2. Heat a grill or skillet over high heat. Cook the meat for 3-5 minutes per side until desired doneness. Remove from the pan and let rest.

3. In the same pan, sauté the bell peppers and onions for 4-5 minutes until softened.

4. Slice the meat thinly against the grain and serve with sautéed peppers and onions, warm tortillas, and toppings.

Lobster Roll

Ingredients:

- 1 lb cooked lobster meat (chopped)
- 1/4 cup mayonnaise
- 1 tbsp lemon juice
- 1 tbsp chopped fresh parsley
- 1/2 tsp Old Bay seasoning (optional)
- Salt and pepper to taste
- 4 soft rolls or hot dog buns
- 2 tbsp melted butter

Instructions:

1. In a bowl, mix lobster meat, mayonnaise, lemon juice, parsley, Old Bay seasoning, salt, and pepper.
2. Lightly toast the rolls with melted butter in a skillet.
3. Spoon the lobster mixture into each roll and serve immediately.

Lamb Kofta with Tzatziki

Ingredients:

For the kofta:

- 1 lb ground lamb
- 1/4 cup chopped onion
- 2 cloves garlic (minced)
- 1 tsp cumin
- 1 tsp coriander
- 1/2 tsp cinnamon
- Salt and pepper to taste
- 1/4 cup chopped parsley

For the tzatziki:

- 1 cup Greek yogurt
- 1/2 cucumber (grated and squeezed dry)
- 1 tbsp lemon juice
- 1 clove garlic (minced)
- 1 tbsp olive oil
- Salt and pepper to taste

Instructions:

1. For the kofta, combine ground lamb, onion, garlic, cumin, coriander, cinnamon, salt, pepper, and parsley. Form into small oval-shaped patties.

2. Grill or pan-fry the koftas over medium-high heat for 3-4 minutes per side until cooked through.

3. For the tzatziki, combine yogurt, cucumber, lemon juice, garlic, olive oil, salt, and pepper in a bowl. Mix well.

4. Serve the koftas with a generous dollop of tzatziki on the side.

Tempura Vegetables

Ingredients:

- 1 zucchini (sliced into sticks)
- 1 sweet potato (peeled and cut into thin fries)
- 1 small onion (sliced into rings)
- 1/2 cup all-purpose flour
- 1/2 cup cornstarch
- 1 egg
- 1 cup cold water (plus more if needed)
- Vegetable oil (for frying)
- Salt to taste

Instructions:

1. Heat oil in a deep pan over medium-high heat for frying.
2. In a bowl, whisk together flour, cornstarch, egg, and cold water to create the batter. It should be light and runny.
3. Dip the vegetables into the batter and carefully lower them into the hot oil. Fry in batches for 2-3 minutes, turning occasionally, until golden and crispy.
4. Drain on paper towels and season with salt.

Sweet and Sour Pork

Ingredients:

For the pork:

- 1 lb pork tenderloin (cut into bite-sized cubes)
- 1/4 cup cornstarch
- 2 tbsp soy sauce
- 2 tbsp vegetable oil

For the sauce:

- 1/4 cup rice vinegar
- 1/4 cup sugar
- 2 tbsp ketchup
- 1 tbsp soy sauce
- 1 tbsp cornstarch (mixed with 2 tbsp water)
- 1 bell pepper (sliced)
- 1/2 onion (sliced)

Instructions:

1. Toss pork cubes in cornstarch until well-coated.
2. Heat vegetable oil in a pan over medium-high heat and cook pork until golden brown. Remove from the pan.
3. In the same pan, add bell pepper, onion, and cook for 2 minutes.

4. In a small bowl, combine rice vinegar, sugar, ketchup, soy sauce, and cornstarch mixture. Pour into the pan and bring to a simmer.

5. Return the pork to the pan and stir to coat in the sauce. Cook for another 2-3 minutes.

6. Serve with rice.

Fish and Chips

Ingredients:

For the fish:

- 4 white fish fillets (cod, haddock, or any firm white fish)
- 1 cup all-purpose flour
- 1 tsp baking powder
- 1/2 tsp salt
- 1 cup cold beer (or sparkling water)
- Vegetable oil (for frying)

For the chips:

- 4 large potatoes (peeled and cut into thick fries)
- Salt to taste

Instructions:

1. Heat oil in a deep pan to 350°F (175°C).
2. For the batter, whisk together flour, baking powder, and salt. Add cold beer and stir until smooth.
3. Dip the fish fillets in the batter and carefully lower them into the hot oil. Fry for 5-7 minutes until golden brown.
4. For the chips, fry the potato fries in the hot oil until crispy, about 4-5 minutes. Drain on paper towels and season with salt.
5. Serve the fish and chips with tartar sauce and lemon wedges.

Chicken Shawarma

Ingredients:

For the marinade:

- 1 lb chicken thighs (boneless, skinless)
- 2 tbsp olive oil
- 1 tbsp garlic (minced)
- 1 tbsp ground cumin
- 1 tbsp paprika
- 1/2 tsp turmeric
- 1/2 tsp cinnamon
- 1/2 tsp ground coriander
- 1/2 tsp ground allspice
- Salt and pepper to taste

For the garlic sauce:

- 1/2 cup mayonnaise
- 2 tbsp garlic (minced)
- 2 tbsp lemon juice
- Salt and pepper to taste

Instructions:

1. Mix olive oil, garlic, cumin, paprika, turmeric, cinnamon, coriander, allspice, salt, and pepper. Marinate the chicken for at least 30 minutes.

2. Cook the chicken on a grill or in a pan over medium heat for 5-7 minutes per side until fully cooked.

3. For the garlic sauce, mix mayonnaise, garlic, lemon juice, salt, and pepper.

4. Serve the chicken on pita bread or in a wrap, drizzled with garlic sauce, and topped with lettuce, tomatoes, and onions.

Grilled Lamb Chops with Mint Yogurt

Ingredients:

For the lamb:

- 8 lamb chops
- 2 tbsp olive oil
- 1 tbsp fresh rosemary (chopped)
- 1 tbsp garlic (minced)
- Salt and pepper to taste

For the mint yogurt:

- 1 cup Greek yogurt
- 2 tbsp fresh mint (chopped)
- 1 tbsp lemon juice
- Salt and pepper to taste

Instructions:

1. Preheat your grill to medium-high heat.
2. Brush lamb chops with olive oil and season with rosemary, garlic, salt, and pepper.
3. Grill the lamb chops for 4-5 minutes per side for medium-rare, or longer to your desired doneness.
4. For the mint yogurt, combine yogurt, mint, lemon juice, salt, and pepper.

5. Serve the lamb chops with a side of mint yogurt.

Jambalaya

Ingredients:

- 1 lb chicken thighs (boneless, skinless, cut into pieces)
- 1 lb andouille sausage (sliced)
- 1 lb shrimp (peeled and deveined)
- 1 onion (chopped)
- 1 bell pepper (chopped)
- 2 stalks celery (chopped)
- 4 cloves garlic (minced)
- 1 (14.5 oz) can diced tomatoes
- 3 cups chicken broth
- 2 cups long-grain rice
- 2 tbsp Cajun seasoning
- 1 tsp thyme
- 1 tsp paprika
- 1/2 tsp cayenne pepper (optional)
- 2 bay leaves
- Salt and pepper to taste
- 2 tbsp olive oil

- Chopped parsley for garnish

Instructions:

1. Heat olive oil in a large pot over medium heat. Add the chicken and sausage and cook until browned. Remove and set aside.

2. In the same pot, add onion, bell pepper, celery, and garlic. Cook until softened, about 5 minutes.

3. Stir in the tomatoes, chicken broth, rice, Cajun seasoning, thyme, paprika, cayenne (if using), and bay leaves. Bring to a boil, then reduce heat to low. Cover and simmer for 20-25 minutes, or until the rice is tender.

4. Add the shrimp and cooked chicken and sausage back into the pot. Stir well, cover, and cook for an additional 5-7 minutes, or until the shrimp are cooked through.

5. Remove bay leaves and discard. Serve with chopped parsley.

Beef Bulgogi

Ingredients:

- 1 lb ribeye or sirloin beef (thinly sliced)
- 1/4 cup soy sauce
- 2 tbsp sesame oil
- 2 tbsp brown sugar
- 1 tbsp rice vinegar
- 4 cloves garlic (minced)
- 1 tbsp ginger (grated)
- 1 tbsp gochujang (Korean chili paste)
- 2 tbsp green onions (chopped)
- 1 tsp sesame seeds
- 1 tbsp vegetable oil (for frying)

Instructions:

1. In a bowl, mix together soy sauce, sesame oil, brown sugar, rice vinegar, garlic, ginger, gochujang, and green onions. Add the sliced beef and marinate for at least 30 minutes (preferably overnight).

2. Heat vegetable oil in a pan over medium-high heat. Add the marinated beef and cook for 3-4 minutes until the beef is cooked through and slightly caramelized.

3. Serve with steamed rice, and garnish with sesame seeds and extra green onions.

Duck Confit with Orange Sauce

Ingredients:

For the duck:

- 4 duck legs
- 4 cups duck fat (or enough to cover the duck legs)
- 2 cloves garlic (minced)
- 1 sprig rosemary
- 1 sprig thyme
- Salt and pepper to taste

For the orange sauce:

- 1 cup orange juice
- 1/2 cup chicken broth
- 1 tbsp orange zest
- 1/4 cup honey
- 2 tbsp butter
- Salt and pepper to taste

Instructions:

1. Preheat the oven to 300°F (150°C). Season the duck legs with salt and pepper.
2. Place the duck legs in a large Dutch oven and cover with duck fat. Add garlic, rosemary, and thyme. Cook in the oven for 2.5-3 hours, until the duck is tender

and the meat easily falls off the bone.

3. For the sauce, combine orange juice, chicken broth, orange zest, and honey in a saucepan. Simmer over medium heat until reduced by half, about 10-15 minutes.

4. Remove from heat, whisk in butter, and season with salt and pepper.

5. To serve, crisp the duck skin in a hot pan for 2-3 minutes. Drizzle the orange sauce over the duck and serve.

Tandoori Chicken

Ingredients:

For the marinade:

- 4 chicken thighs (bone-in, skinless)
- 1 cup plain yogurt
- 2 tbsp lemon juice
- 1 tbsp ginger (grated)
- 1 tbsp garlic (minced)
- 1 tbsp ground cumin
- 1 tbsp ground coriander
- 1 tbsp paprika
- 1 tsp turmeric
- 1 tsp garam masala
- 1/2 tsp cayenne pepper
- Salt to taste

Instructions:

1. In a bowl, mix all marinade ingredients. Add the chicken thighs and coat well. Marinate for at least 2 hours, preferably overnight.

2. Preheat the oven to 400°F (200°C). Place the chicken on a rack over a baking sheet.

3. Bake for 30-35 minutes, or until the chicken reaches an internal temperature of 165°F (75°C).

4. Serve with rice and naan bread.

Peking Duck

Ingredients:

- 1 whole duck (about 5 lbs)
- 2 tbsp honey
- 2 tbsp soy sauce
- 2 tbsp rice vinegar
- 1 tbsp Chinese five-spice powder
- 1 tbsp hoisin sauce
- 6-8 thin pancakes or Mandarin pancakes
- 1 cucumber (sliced thin)
- 2-3 green onions (sliced thin)

Instructions:

1. Preheat the oven to 375°F (190°C).
2. Rinse the duck and pat dry. Rub the duck with five-spice powder and season with salt. Place the duck on a roasting rack.
3. Mix honey, soy sauce, rice vinegar, and hoisin sauce. Brush the mixture over the duck.
4. Roast the duck for 1.5-2 hours, basting occasionally, until the skin is crispy and golden.
5. Slice the duck thinly and serve with pancakes, cucumber, green onions, and extra hoisin sauce.

Korean BBQ Beef

Ingredients:

- 1 lb beef short ribs (or flank steak)
- 1/4 cup soy sauce
- 2 tbsp sesame oil
- 2 tbsp brown sugar
- 2 tbsp rice vinegar
- 2 cloves garlic (minced)
- 1 tsp ginger (grated)
- 2 tbsp green onions (chopped)
- 1 tbsp sesame seeds

Instructions:

1. In a bowl, mix soy sauce, sesame oil, brown sugar, rice vinegar, garlic, and ginger. Add the beef and marinate for at least 30 minutes.
2. Grill or pan-fry the beef for 3-5 minutes per side, depending on thickness, until cooked to desired doneness.
3. Serve with rice, garnished with green onions and sesame seeds.

Moussaka

Ingredients:

- 1 lb ground lamb (or beef)
- 1 onion (chopped)
- 2 cloves garlic (minced)
- 2 cups tomato sauce
- 1/2 tsp cinnamon
- 1/2 tsp nutmeg
- 1/2 tsp oregano
- 3 eggplants (sliced)
- 2 cups béchamel sauce (recipe below)
- 1/4 cup grated Parmesan

For the béchamel sauce:

- 4 tbsp butter
- 1/4 cup flour
- 2 cups milk
- Salt and pepper to taste
- 1/4 tsp nutmeg

Instructions:

1. Preheat the oven to 375°F (190°C).

2. Sauté ground meat, onion, and garlic until browned. Add tomato sauce, cinnamon, nutmeg, and oregano. Simmer for 15 minutes.

3. Grill or fry eggplant slices until soft.

4. For the béchamel sauce, melt butter in a saucepan, whisk in flour, and gradually add milk. Stir until thickened. Season with salt, pepper, and nutmeg.

5. Layer the meat sauce, eggplant, and béchamel sauce in a baking dish. Top with Parmesan.

6. Bake for 30-40 minutes until golden and bubbly.

Paella

Ingredients:

- 1 lb chicken thighs (cut into pieces)
- 1 lb shrimp (peeled and deveined)
- 1/2 lb chorizo (sliced)
- 1 onion (chopped)
- 1 bell pepper (chopped)
- 2 cups Arborio rice
- 4 cups chicken broth
- 1/2 tsp saffron threads
- 1 tsp paprika
- 2 cloves garlic (minced)
- 1 cup frozen peas
- 2 tbsp olive oil
- Salt and pepper to taste
- Lemon wedges for garnish

Instructions:

1. Heat olive oil in a large skillet over medium heat. Brown the chicken and chorizo. Remove from the pan and set aside.
2. In the same pan, sauté onion, bell pepper, and garlic until softened.

3. Add rice and cook for 2 minutes. Add saffron, paprika, chicken broth, and bring to a simmer.

4. Stir in peas, chicken, chorizo, and shrimp. Cover and cook for 15-20 minutes, or until rice is tender and liquid is absorbed.

5. Garnish with lemon wedges and serve.

Crab Cakes with Lemon Aioli

Ingredients:

For the crab cakes:

- 1 lb fresh crab meat
- 1/2 cup breadcrumbs
- 1/4 cup mayonnaise
- 1 egg
- 2 tbsp Dijon mustard
- 1 tbsp lemon juice
- 2 tbsp parsley (chopped)
- Salt and pepper to taste
- 2 tbsp olive oil (for frying)

For the lemon aioli:

- 1/2 cup mayonnaise
- 1 tbsp lemon juice
- 1 tsp lemon zest
- 1 garlic clove (minced)
- Salt and pepper to taste

Instructions:

1. For the aioli, mix all ingredients in a bowl and set aside.

2. Combine crab meat, breadcrumbs, mayonnaise, egg, mustard, lemon juice, parsley, salt, and pepper. Form into patties.

3. Heat olive oil in a skillet over medium heat. Fry the crab cakes for 3-4 minutes per side, until golden and crispy.

4. Serve the crab cakes with the lemon aioli.

Chicken Parmesan

Ingredients:

- 4 boneless, skinless chicken breasts
- 1 cup all-purpose flour
- 2 large eggs (beaten)
- 1 cup breadcrumbs
- 1/2 cup grated Parmesan cheese
- 2 cups marinara sauce
- 1 cup shredded mozzarella cheese
- 1/4 cup fresh basil (chopped)
- Olive oil for frying
- Salt and pepper to taste

Instructions:

1. Preheat the oven to 375°F (190°C).
2. Season the chicken breasts with salt and pepper.
3. Dredge the chicken in flour, dip it into the beaten eggs, and then coat it with the breadcrumb and Parmesan mixture.
4. Heat olive oil in a skillet over medium heat. Fry the chicken breasts for 3-4 minutes on each side, until golden brown. Transfer to a baking dish.
5. Pour marinara sauce over the chicken breasts, and top with shredded mozzarella cheese.

6. Bake for 20-25 minutes, or until the cheese is melted and bubbly.

7. Garnish with fresh basil and serve with pasta or a side salad.

Grilled Octopus with Lemon

Ingredients:

- 2 lbs octopus (whole or tentacles)
- 1/4 cup olive oil
- 1 lemon (zested and juiced)
- 2 cloves garlic (minced)
- 1 tbsp fresh parsley (chopped)
- Salt and pepper to taste

Instructions:

1. Preheat the grill to medium-high heat.
2. Bring a large pot of salted water to a boil. Add the octopus and cook for 45-60 minutes, or until tender. Drain and let it cool.
3. Once cool, cut the tentacles into smaller pieces if desired.
4. In a bowl, mix olive oil, lemon juice, lemon zest, garlic, parsley, salt, and pepper.
5. Brush the octopus pieces with the marinade and let them sit for 10-15 minutes.
6. Grill the octopus for 3-4 minutes per side, until slightly charred.
7. Serve with additional lemon wedges and garnish with parsley.

Thai Green Curry

Ingredients:

- 1 lb chicken (sliced into strips)
- 1 can (14 oz) coconut milk
- 2 tbsp green curry paste
- 1 tbsp fish sauce
- 1 tbsp brown sugar
- 1 bell pepper (sliced)
- 1 zucchini (sliced)
- 1 cup mushrooms (sliced)
- 1/2 cup basil (chopped)
- 1 tbsp vegetable oil
- Salt and pepper to taste
- Jasmine rice for serving

Instructions:

1. Heat oil in a large skillet or wok over medium heat. Add chicken and cook until browned. Remove and set aside.
2. In the same skillet, add green curry paste and cook for 1-2 minutes until fragrant.
3. Add coconut milk, fish sauce, brown sugar, and bring to a simmer.

4. Add the bell pepper, zucchini, mushrooms, and cooked chicken. Simmer for 10-15 minutes, until the vegetables are tender.

5. Season with salt and pepper. Garnish with fresh basil.

6. Serve with steamed jasmine rice.

Stuffed Grape Leaves

Ingredients:

- 1 jar grape leaves (drained and rinsed)
- 1 cup rice (washed)
- 1 lb ground lamb (or beef)
- 1 onion (finely chopped)
- 2 tbsp olive oil
- 1 tsp dried mint
- 1 tsp allspice
- 1/2 tsp cinnamon
- 2 tbsp lemon juice
- Salt and pepper to taste

Instructions:

1. In a skillet, heat olive oil and sauté onion until softened. Add the ground meat and cook until browned.

2. Stir in rice, mint, allspice, cinnamon, salt, and pepper. Add 2 cups of water and cook until the rice is half-done, about 8 minutes. Let it cool.

3. Lay a grape leaf flat, and place a spoonful of the filling near the stem. Fold in the sides and roll tightly to form a small parcel.

4. Arrange the stuffed grape leaves in a large pot, layering them carefully.

5. Pour lemon juice and enough water to cover the grape leaves. Place a plate on top to keep them submerged.

6. Bring to a boil, reduce heat, and simmer for 45-60 minutes until tender.

7. Serve warm or at room temperature.

Beef Wellington

Ingredients:

- 2 lb beef tenderloin (center-cut)
- 2 tbsp olive oil
- 2 tbsp Dijon mustard
- 1 lb mushrooms (finely chopped)
- 1/2 cup pate (optional)
- 1 package puff pastry (enough to wrap the beef)
- 1 egg (beaten, for egg wash)
- Salt and pepper to taste

Instructions:

1. Preheat the oven to 400°F (200°C).
2. Heat olive oil in a skillet over high heat. Sear the beef tenderloin on all sides for 3-4 minutes. Let it cool, then brush with Dijon mustard.
3. In the same skillet, cook the mushrooms until all moisture has evaporated. Let the mushroom mixture cool.
4. Roll out the puff pastry on a floured surface. Spread pate (if using) over the pastry and top with the mushroom mixture.
5. Place the beef on the pastry and wrap it tightly. Seal the edges and brush with egg wash.
6. Bake for 35-40 minutes, or until the pastry is golden brown and the beef reaches your desired doneness.

7. Let rest for 10 minutes before slicing. Serve with your favorite side dishes.

Shrimp Scampi

Ingredients:

- 1 lb large shrimp (peeled and deveined)
- 8 oz spaghetti or linguine
- 4 cloves garlic (minced)
- 1/2 cup dry white wine
- 1/4 cup lemon juice
- 1/4 cup unsalted butter
- 1/4 cup olive oil
- 1/4 cup fresh parsley (chopped)
- Salt and pepper to taste

Instructions:

1. Cook the pasta according to package instructions. Reserve 1/2 cup of pasta water.
2. Heat olive oil and butter in a large skillet over medium heat. Add garlic and cook until fragrant, about 1 minute.
3. Add shrimp to the skillet and cook for 2-3 minutes per side until pink.
4. Stir in the wine and lemon juice, simmer for 2-3 minutes to reduce the sauce slightly.
5. Add the cooked pasta to the skillet, toss to combine, and add reserved pasta water to reach the desired sauce consistency.

6. Season with salt and pepper. Garnish with parsley and serve immediately.

Chimichurri Steak

Ingredients:

- 2 ribeye steaks (or your choice of cut)
- Salt and pepper to taste

For the chimichurri:

- 1 cup fresh parsley (chopped)
- 1/4 cup red wine vinegar
- 2 tbsp olive oil
- 2 cloves garlic (minced)
- 1/2 tsp red pepper flakes
- Salt and pepper to taste

Instructions:

1. Preheat your grill or grill pan to medium-high heat.
2. Season the steaks with salt and pepper and grill to your desired doneness (about 4-5 minutes per side for medium).
3. In a bowl, combine parsley, vinegar, olive oil, garlic, red pepper flakes, salt, and pepper.
4. Once the steaks are cooked, top with chimichurri sauce and serve with a side of vegetables or potatoes.

Lamb Tagine

Ingredients:

- 1.5 lbs lamb (shoulder or shank, cut into pieces)
- 1 onion (chopped)
- 2 cloves garlic (minced)
- 1 tbsp ground cumin
- 1 tbsp ground coriander
- 1 tbsp ground cinnamon
- 1 tsp turmeric
- 2 cups beef or lamb broth
- 1 can (14 oz) diced tomatoes
- 1/2 cup dried apricots (chopped)
- 1/4 cup almonds (toasted)
- Olive oil for browning
- Salt and pepper to taste
- Fresh cilantro for garnish

Instructions:

1. Heat olive oil in a tagine or large pot over medium-high heat. Brown the lamb pieces in batches, then remove and set aside.
2. In the same pot, sauté onion and garlic until softened.

3. Stir in cumin, coriander, cinnamon, turmeric, salt, and pepper. Add broth, tomatoes, and lamb.

4. Bring to a simmer, cover, and cook for 1.5 to 2 hours, until the lamb is tender.

5. Stir in apricots and cook for an additional 10 minutes. Garnish with toasted almonds and cilantro.

6. Serve with couscous or flatbread.

Chicken Kiev

Ingredients:

- 4 boneless, skinless chicken breasts
- 1/2 cup unsalted butter (softened)
- 4 cloves garlic (minced)
- 2 tbsp fresh parsley (chopped)
- 1 tbsp fresh dill (chopped)
- 1 tbsp lemon juice
- Salt and pepper to taste
- 1/2 cup flour
- 2 large eggs (beaten)
- 1 cup breadcrumbs
- Vegetable oil for frying

Instructions:

1. In a bowl, combine butter, garlic, parsley, dill, lemon juice, salt, and pepper. Roll the butter into a log and refrigerate until firm.

2. Flatten the chicken breasts using a mallet and season with salt and pepper. Place a portion of the herb butter inside each chicken breast and fold the chicken around the butter.

3. Dredge the chicken in flour, dip in egg, and coat in breadcrumbs.

4. Heat oil in a pan over medium heat. Fry the chicken for 5-6 minutes per side, until golden brown and cooked through.

5. Serve immediately with mashed potatoes or a salad.

Baked Ziti

Ingredients:

- 1 lb ziti pasta
- 2 cups marinara sauce
- 1 lb ricotta cheese
- 2 cups shredded mozzarella cheese
- 1/2 cup grated Parmesan cheese
- 1 tbsp fresh basil (chopped)
- Salt and pepper to taste

Instructions:

1. Preheat the oven to 350°F (175°C).
2. Cook ziti according to package instructions. Drain and return to the pot.
3. Mix marinara sauce, ricotta cheese, half of the mozzarella, and Parmesan cheese. Season with salt and pepper.
4. Transfer the pasta mixture to a baking dish. Top with the remaining mozzarella cheese.
5. Bake for 20-25 minutes, until the cheese is melted and bubbly.
6. Garnish with fresh basil and serve hot.

Risotto with Porcini Mushrooms

Ingredients:

- 1 cup Arborio rice
- 1/2 cup dried porcini mushrooms (rehydrated in warm water)
- 4 cups chicken or vegetable broth (kept warm)
- 1/2 cup dry white wine
- 1/2 cup Parmesan cheese (grated)
- 1 small onion (finely chopped)
- 2 cloves garlic (minced)
- 2 tbsp butter
- 1 tbsp olive oil
- Salt and pepper to taste
- Fresh parsley for garnish

Instructions:

1. In a large pan, heat the olive oil and butter over medium heat. Add the onion and garlic, and sauté until softened, about 3-4 minutes.
2. Add the rehydrated porcini mushrooms (reserve the liquid) and sauté for another 2-3 minutes.
3. Stir in the Arborio rice and cook for 2 minutes until lightly toasted.
4. Add the white wine and cook until mostly absorbed.

5. Begin adding the warm broth, one ladle at a time, stirring constantly and allowing each addition to be absorbed before adding the next.

6. Continue this process for 18-20 minutes, until the rice is creamy and tender.

7. Stir in the Parmesan cheese, and season with salt and pepper.

8. Serve the risotto garnished with fresh parsley.

Porchetta

Ingredients:

- 4 lb pork belly (with skin on)
- 2 tbsp olive oil
- 1 tbsp rosemary (chopped)
- 1 tbsp thyme (chopped)
- 4 cloves garlic (minced)
- 1 tsp fennel seeds
- Zest of 1 lemon
- Salt and pepper to taste

Instructions:

1. Preheat the oven to 375°F (190°C).
2. Score the pork belly skin in a crisscross pattern. Rub the pork with olive oil, rosemary, thyme, garlic, fennel seeds, lemon zest, salt, and pepper.
3. Roll the pork belly into a tight roast and secure with kitchen twine.
4. Place the porchetta on a roasting rack in a pan, skin-side up. Roast for 2-2.5 hours, or until the skin is golden and crispy.
5. Let the porchetta rest for 10-15 minutes before slicing and serving.

Lobster Bisque

Ingredients:

- 2 lobster tails (cooked and chopped)
- 4 cups seafood stock
- 1/2 cup heavy cream
- 1/4 cup brandy
- 1 small onion (chopped)
- 2 cloves garlic (minced)
- 1 celery stalk (chopped)
- 1 medium carrot (chopped)
- 1 tbsp tomato paste
- 2 tbsp butter
- 1 tbsp flour
- Salt and pepper to taste

Instructions:

1. In a large pot, melt butter over medium heat. Add the onion, garlic, celery, and carrot, and sauté for 5-7 minutes, until softened.

2. Stir in the tomato paste and cook for 1 minute. Add the flour and cook for 2 minutes, stirring constantly to form a roux.

3. Gradually add the seafood stock, whisking constantly to prevent lumps. Bring the soup to a simmer and cook for 10-15 minutes.

4. Add the brandy and continue to simmer for another 5 minutes.

5. Blend the soup using an immersion blender or regular blender until smooth.

6. Stir in the heavy cream and chopped lobster meat. Cook for another 5 minutes until heated through.

7. Season with salt and pepper. Serve hot, garnished with extra lobster pieces.

Prawn Ceviche

Ingredients:

- 1 lb raw shrimp (peeled, deveined, and chopped)
- 1 cup fresh lime juice
- 1/2 cup fresh orange juice
- 1 small red onion (thinly sliced)
- 1 small cucumber (diced)
- 1 tomato (diced)
- 1 avocado (diced)
- 1/4 cup fresh cilantro (chopped)
- 1-2 jalapeños (diced)
- Salt and pepper to taste

Instructions:

1. Place the chopped shrimp in a large bowl and cover with lime and orange juice. Let it sit in the refrigerator for 1-2 hours, or until the shrimp turns pink from the citrus juice (this is the "cooking" process).

2. Add the onion, cucumber, tomato, avocado, cilantro, and jalapeños to the shrimp mixture.

3. Toss to combine and season with salt and pepper to taste.

4. Serve chilled with tortilla chips or on tostadas.

Tofu Stir-Fry

Ingredients:

- 1 block firm tofu (drained and pressed)
- 2 tbsp vegetable oil
- 1 bell pepper (sliced)
- 1 onion (sliced)
- 1 zucchini (sliced)
- 2 cloves garlic (minced)
- 1 tbsp ginger (grated)
- 3 tbsp soy sauce
- 1 tbsp sesame oil
- 1 tsp rice vinegar
- 1 tbsp honey (optional)
- 1/4 cup green onions (chopped)
- Sesame seeds for garnish

Instructions:

1. Cut the tofu into cubes and sauté in a large pan or wok with 1 tbsp vegetable oil over medium-high heat. Cook for 5-7 minutes, until golden brown on all sides. Remove tofu from the pan and set aside.

2. In the same pan, add the remaining oil and sauté the bell pepper, onion, zucchini, garlic, and ginger for 5-7 minutes until tender.

3. Stir in soy sauce, sesame oil, rice vinegar, and honey (if using). Return the tofu to the pan and toss to combine.

4. Cook for another 2-3 minutes, then garnish with green onions and sesame seeds.

5. Serve with steamed rice.

Grilled Vegetable Skewers

Ingredients:

- 1 red bell pepper (cut into chunks)
- 1 zucchini (sliced)
- 1 yellow squash (sliced)
- 1 red onion (cut into chunks)
- 1 cup cherry tomatoes
- 2 tbsp olive oil
- 1 tbsp balsamic vinegar
- 1 tsp dried oregano
- Salt and pepper to taste

Instructions:

1. Preheat the grill to medium-high heat.
2. In a bowl, combine olive oil, balsamic vinegar, oregano, salt, and pepper. Toss the vegetables in the marinade and let them sit for 10-15 minutes.
3. Thread the vegetables onto skewers, alternating them for a colorful mix.
4. Grill the skewers for 8-10 minutes, turning occasionally, until the vegetables are tender and slightly charred.
5. Serve with a drizzle of olive oil or your favorite dipping sauce.

Pulled Pork Sandwiches

Ingredients:

- 4 lb pork shoulder
- 1/4 cup brown sugar
- 2 tbsp paprika
- 1 tbsp garlic powder
- 1 tbsp onion powder
- 1 tsp ground cumin
- 1 tsp ground black pepper
- 1/2 tsp salt
- 2 cups barbecue sauce
- 8 sandwich buns

Instructions:

1. Preheat the oven to 300°F (150°C).
2. In a bowl, mix brown sugar, paprika, garlic powder, onion powder, cumin, pepper, and salt.
3. Rub the spice mixture over the pork shoulder. Place the pork in a roasting pan and cover with foil.
4. Roast for 5-6 hours, or until the pork is tender and shreds easily with a fork.
5. Remove the pork from the pan and shred with forks. Mix the shredded pork with barbecue sauce.

6. Serve the pulled pork on sandwich buns with additional barbecue sauce if desired.

Spaghetti Carbonara

Ingredients:

- 1 lb spaghetti
- 4 oz pancetta (diced)
- 2 large eggs
- 1/2 cup grated Parmesan cheese
- 1/4 cup heavy cream (optional)
- 2 cloves garlic (minced)
- Salt and pepper to taste
- Fresh parsley for garnish

Instructions:

1. Cook the spaghetti according to package instructions. Reserve 1/2 cup pasta water before draining.
2. In a skillet, sauté pancetta over medium heat until crispy. Remove from heat and set aside.
3. In a bowl, whisk together eggs, Parmesan, and heavy cream (if using). Season with salt and pepper.
4. Add the cooked pasta to the pancetta skillet and toss to combine.
5. Quickly pour the egg mixture over the pasta, tossing to coat and creating a creamy sauce. If the sauce is too thick, add a little reserved pasta water.
6. Serve with fresh parsley and extra Parmesan.

Veal Piccata

Ingredients:

- 4 veal cutlets
- 1/2 cup all-purpose flour
- 1/4 cup olive oil
- 1/4 cup lemon juice
- 1/4 cup white wine
- 2 tbsp capers
- 2 tbsp butter
- Salt and pepper to taste
- Fresh parsley for garnish

Instructions:

1. Season the veal cutlets with salt and pepper, then dredge them in flour, shaking off the excess.

2. Heat olive oil in a skillet over medium-high heat. Cook the veal for 2-3 minutes per side until golden brown and cooked through. Remove the veal from the skillet.

3. In the same skillet, add lemon juice, white wine, and capers, scraping up any brown bits. Cook for 2-3 minutes, then stir in butter to form a sauce.

4. Return the veal to the skillet and coat with the sauce.

5. Serve with the sauce drizzled over the veal and garnished with parsley.

Chili Crab

Ingredients:

- 2 lbs whole crabs (or crab legs)
- 1 tbsp vegetable oil
- 2 cloves garlic (minced)
- 1-inch piece ginger (minced)
- 1-2 red chilies (sliced)
- 1 tbsp tomato paste
- 1/4 cup ketchup
- 2 tbsp soy sauce
- 2 tbsp rice vinegar
- 1 tbsp sugar
- 1/2 cup chicken broth
- 1 tbsp corn starch (optional, to thicken)
- 2 green onions (chopped)
- Fresh cilantro for garnish

Instructions:

1. Heat vegetable oil in a large pan or wok over medium heat. Add garlic, ginger, and red chilies, sautéing for 2 minutes until fragrant.

2. Add tomato paste and cook for another minute. Stir in ketchup, soy sauce, rice vinegar, sugar, and chicken broth. Bring the sauce to a simmer.

3. Add the crabs and cover, cooking for 10-12 minutes (or until the crabs are fully cooked if using whole crabs).

4. If the sauce needs thickening, dissolve corn starch in a little water and stir it into the sauce, cooking for 2-3 more minutes.

5. Garnish with green onions and cilantro before serving with steamed rice or crusty bread.

Beef Rendang

Ingredients:

- 2 lbs beef chuck (cut into chunks)
- 2 tbsp vegetable oil
- 1 onion (chopped)
- 3 cloves garlic (minced)
- 1-inch piece ginger (minced)
- 1 stalk lemongrass (smashed)
- 3-4 dried red chilies (soaked and chopped)
- 1 tsp turmeric powder
- 1 tsp ground cumin
- 1 tsp ground coriander
- 1 can (14 oz) coconut milk
- 1/4 cup beef broth
- 2 tbsp tamarind paste
- 1 tbsp brown sugar
- Salt to taste
- Fresh cilantro for garnish

Instructions:

1. Heat the vegetable oil in a large pot over medium heat. Add the onion, garlic, ginger, and lemongrass, sautéing for 5-7 minutes until softened.

2. Stir in the chopped chilies, turmeric, cumin, and coriander, and cook for another 2 minutes.

3. Add the beef chunks and sear until browned on all sides.

4. Pour in the coconut milk, beef broth, tamarind paste, and brown sugar. Bring to a simmer, then reduce the heat to low.

5. Cover and simmer for 2-3 hours, stirring occasionally, until the beef is tender and the sauce has thickened.

6. Season with salt to taste and garnish with fresh cilantro before serving with rice.

Baked Cod with Lemon and Capers

Ingredients:

- 4 cod fillets (about 6 oz each)
- 2 tbsp olive oil
- 1 lemon (sliced)
- 2 tbsp capers (drained)
- 2 cloves garlic (minced)
- 1/4 cup white wine
- Salt and pepper to taste
- Fresh parsley for garnish

Instructions:

1. Preheat the oven to 375°F (190°C).
2. Place the cod fillets in a baking dish. Drizzle with olive oil and season with salt and pepper.
3. Scatter lemon slices, capers, and garlic around the fish.
4. Pour white wine over the fillets and bake for 15-20 minutes, or until the fish is opaque and easily flakes with a fork.
5. Garnish with fresh parsley before serving with roasted vegetables or a light salad.

Pappardelle with Duck Ragu

Ingredients:

- 1 lb pappardelle pasta
- 2 tbsp olive oil
- 2 duck legs (skin on)
- 1 onion (chopped)
- 2 cloves garlic (minced)
- 1 carrot (chopped)
- 2 celery stalks (chopped)
- 1 cup red wine
- 2 cups chicken or beef broth
- 1 tbsp tomato paste
- 1 bay leaf
- 1 tsp fresh thyme (or 1/2 tsp dried thyme)
- Salt and pepper to taste
- Fresh Parmesan for serving

Instructions:

1. Heat olive oil in a large pot over medium heat. Season the duck legs with salt and pepper, and brown them on both sides. Remove the duck and set aside.

2. In the same pot, add onion, garlic, carrot, and celery. Sauté for 5-7 minutes until softened.

3. Stir in tomato paste, and cook for 2 minutes. Add red wine and simmer for 5 minutes, scraping up any browned bits from the pot.

4. Return the duck legs to the pot, and pour in the broth. Add bay leaf, thyme, salt, and pepper.

5. Cover and simmer for 2-3 hours, or until the duck is tender and the meat can be easily shredded.

6. Remove the duck legs, shred the meat, and discard the bones. Return the shredded meat to the sauce.

7. Cook the pappardelle pasta according to package instructions. Toss the pasta with the duck ragu and serve with grated Parmesan.

Sautéed Scallops with Garlic Butter

Ingredients:

- 12 large scallops (fresh or thawed)
- 2 tbsp butter
- 2 cloves garlic (minced)
- 1 tbsp lemon juice
- 1 tbsp olive oil
- Salt and pepper to taste
- Fresh parsley for garnish

Instructions:

1. Pat the scallops dry with paper towels. Season with salt and pepper.
2. Heat olive oil and butter in a large skillet over medium-high heat.
3. Add the scallops and cook for 2-3 minutes per side, or until golden brown and cooked through. Be careful not to overcook them.
4. Remove the scallops from the pan and set aside. In the same pan, add garlic and sauté for 1-2 minutes until fragrant.
5. Stir in lemon juice and any remaining butter. Pour the garlic butter over the scallops.
6. Garnish with fresh parsley and serve with a side of vegetables or pasta.

www.ingramcontent.com/pod-product-compliance
Lightning Source LLC
LaVergne TN
LVHW081611060526
838201LV00054B/2192